ANCHOR
BOOKS

A SLICE OF LIFE

Edited by

Rachael Radford

First published in Great Britain in 2003 by
ANCHOR BOOKS
Remus House,
Coltsfoot Drive,
Peterborough, PE2 9JX
Telephone (01733) 898102

HB ISBN 1 84418 088 3
SB ISBN 1 84418 089 1

The Old City Of Durham

On Page 76

Written By:-

Susan Carole Gash-Roberts

FOREWORD

Anchor Books is a small press, established in 1992, with the aim of promoting readable poetry to as wide an audience as possible.

We hope to establish an outlet for writers of poetry who may have struggled to see their work in print.

The poems presented here have been selected from many entries, and as always editing proved to be a difficult task.

I trust this selection will delight and please the authors and all those who enjoy reading poetry.

Rachael Radford
Editor

CONTENTS

IN THE VALLEY OF DREAMS WHERE WE MEET

Garlands of flowers
At our feet
The tendrils of our love
Entwined in passions sweet

In the valley of dreams
Where we meet

Holding, touching, caressing, loving
Under a multi-coloured sky
Showered by warm scented beams
Of love's sweet cry

The delight of love's sweet
Mysteries unfold
In delights of fantasy untold

The ebb and flow together brings
Like the softness of a butterfly's wings
As rising passions complete
In the valley of dreams where we meet

David Stuart

OLD ARTHUR ITUS

Arthur Itus is a name close to me
He's in my back, my hips, and my one bad knee
He prevents me from dancing, and kneeling down on the ground
Life is not easy when he's around
I dose him with tablets and try to keep fit
When I get tired, I sit down and knit
There are many, many people, who carry this pain
Why we have to put up with it, just seems insane
You can always spot us as we walk down the street
We all walk sort of crab-like, and when we stop to speak
We lean on our sticks or one hand on the wall
We compare our medications, and how we cope
Then carry on, now feeling more hope
John knows old Arthur Itus too, not just me
He's currently waiting to get a new knee
He has a new hip, that's been just great
Even if he had a while to wait
Now one of my knees, has kicked old Arthur out
I have a full new knee, the Consultant told me about
It's three years now since I got my knee of steel
I had the op, no trouble, nothing did I feel
On the x-ray plate, it's plain to see
Two metal plates, where my bones used to be
Half of my knee cap has been taken away
To anyone considering, all I can say
If the big man says yes, don't hesitate
Put your name on the list, and patiently wait

Elizabeth

DRIFTING PETALS

Your love I know is fading
For your passion is beginning to cool
I sense that away you are drifting
Like petals on a pool

Your arms are no longer clinging
At my touch I feel you freeze
You are floating quietly away, falling
Like petals in the breeze

Your lips have lost their burning
My life is now an empty dream
As your love flows away, swirling
Like petals in a stream

Our love is now over, dying
To hope, is to be a fool
I know that you are gone forever
Like petals sinking in a pool

Derek Bradley

GLOBAL WARRING

When ghastly gargoyles grind out Heaven's tears,
Fiery fountains foaming fauna fling,
Raging rivers rise to rupture rocks,
Who'll teach the dove a different song to sing?

When earthen crust corrupts the cheating charts,
Nimbus nods to never-ending night,
The globe of blue basks blearily in black,
Can man survive his purple, perilous plight?

If so; what's etched in stone will echo loud;
Those basic rules, the path to Heaven above;
A guiding light God gave to rich and poor;
His ten commands through which to channel love.

Brenda Mentha

EMPATHY

When the walls of your mind –
Go rocketing through your soul,
There will be empathy.
When your life falls to pieces –
Right before your eyes,
I will stand right by you.

When you feel alone in the crowd,
When your brain is beating loud,
When all seems lost, when silence is strong,
I will lift you up tall to the place where you belong.

Empathy is something not in short supply,
Because I suffered for everyone,
And I knew I was going to die.
So when you're endangered by life,
I will love you while the sun shines on –
Shines on distant lands.

I will show you the holes in my hands,
And comfort your soul.

God is good! Heaven sings.
God is good! Cos goodness he brings.

Empathy.

Simon P Jones

UNRAVEL

One life in the palm of our hand,
Every day seems like an eternity,
Trying to find the truth, trying to understand,
Why one life is full of kindness and such pity.

After you reach a certain age,
The clock starts spinning, really fast,
And you realise you're locked inside the cage,
Of life that will soon come to pass.

Turn a minute into an hour, or day,
Treasure every single emotion, truth or inexplicable kindness,
The bad will always come with the good, that's nature's way,
Until you slowly begin to unravel life's little mess.

Kimberly Harries

THE SILENCE OF BARKINGSIDE
(The 25th anniversary edition)

Pretending to feel no more than good friends, we parted,
a farewell drink, but why did we feel so down-hearted?
Too afraid to speak of love, we imprisoned our fate,
love seemed so impossible in that year of seventy-eight.

Pretending to feel no more than good friends, we kissed,
farewell tidings, yet not a word of love or being missed.
Too afraid to speak of sorrow, made silent this goodbye,
but on leaving Barkingside, did I see a tear fill your eye?

Pretending to feel no more than good friends, we waved,
hundreds of miles must part us, and love's call betrayed.
Too afraid to speak of passion, forged this last farewell,
until the silence of Barkingside, finds voice in us to tell.

Keith Leese

JUST TOM

I was born Thomas but named just Tom
In a small village in Middlesex I came from
This said village was named Isleworth long time
Ago, in fact 85 years this month of September
The 27th to be exact, I can remember
Not that year of 1917, no way a baby was I
But lots of memories come back so I will try
To put it down in verse, no way will I lie
Loving poetry as I do, typing such poems I love
Not 100 not 200 but eight, you bet
You could say poetry comes out of my ears, so get
Set to receive more about love and peace, sign of the dove
Just give me a subject of any kind, a poem you will get okay
Not any Tom, Dick or Harry, but a poet, well I do thus say
A war veteran of the Second World War, a small part to play
That's my lot this time, close this poem with God Bless
To win your award in the top 100 – I do my very best

T Sexton

A PATTERN FOR LIVING!

See all things, with a positive view
while leaving an abundance of room,
for pleasures to bud - prosper and bloom.
Learn to find pleasure spontaneously even in sonic boom,
Thereby dispelling the doldrums
a sparkle and sheen - as in tune.

Make good of all that occurs
embracing every circumstance,
Taking its constraints - two fold
your life to emancipate and enhance.
Causing others still to stare
while taking a second glance,
but now a stare in pleasure
as your life, steadfastly goes in advance.

Always gain the upper hand
attain the reins, be bold,
being pleasant, not obnoxious
being in control - not controlled.
Not taking yourself - or life
too deep, too strenuous or serious.
Never letting others set your standards
and above all else be yourself - spontaneous.

Avoid all that causes unhappiness
the gripes and moans - begrudgers,
as hate - vengeance spells disaster
always avoid their constraints and slurs.
Don't harbour misgivings - apprehensions
reward all aims and goals achieved,
sight the obvious, as seen and heard
above all else - never be self-deceived.

Gary J Finlay

FOREVER WAITING!

You blew a scented little kiss
    I knew it was from you
Telling me how you missed
    My company providing you were true
I blush to think you care for me
    As now I eagerly await
To hear your footsteps in the lane
    As I wait at the gate

Footsteps and there are many
    But never yours my love
In the lane patiently waiting
    For my handsome dove
I wait and grow impatient
    Getting cross you don't have a mind
Leaving me alone like this
    How could you be unkind?

I received an urgent message
    Oh dear! A sad tale more than woe
You had met with an accident
    This was the severest blow
Never regaining consciousness
    You simply passed away
Leaving me to mourn and pine
    In that lane many years ago
Still hearing your footsteps
    As you come to me
I still reach out to greet you
    In all that invisibility

R D Hiscoke

WHERE DO I START?

Saying things, being good,
doing this, as I know I should.
Remembering things that we used to do,
when we were kids, me and you,
You promised you would never hurt me, now
you have torn me apart,
Leaving me to pick up the pieces, not knowing
where to start.

Carry on the same, you say,
it's just another day,
Typical, it's you that is ill, but still
think of us,
And you say get behind my family, please don't
make any fuss,
But, if that is what you want,
that's how it will be.
You are my brother, all that's left of the family.
I know we can't live forever, and wouldn't
want to anyway,
So what we have now, we will treasure,
a bonus every day.

Maureen Arnold

ALONE AGAIN

No more texting, oh happy sound,
Baggy knickers, he won't pop round!
Legs all hairy, feeling sad,
Alone again, feeling mad.

No more piles of clothes in heap,
Delete all messages, none to keep.
Friends are back, men are out,
Alone again, feeling doubt.

Comfort eating, no need to slim,
Watching telly, stuff the gym,
Why did I do it, sell my soul?
Alone again, a big black hole.

Wonder how it all went wrong,
Lasted weeks, but felt so long,
Head held high, will show no shame,
Alone again, no one to blame.

Missing all the sexual tension,
Chatting on the phone extension,
Reading thoughts and praying hard,
Alone again, lost my guard.

Seeing through the blindness now,
Wishing that we'd had that row,
I should have waited, played it hard,
Alone again, feeling scarred.

No more chances, got it wrong,
No more dreaming, to that song,
It's all over, wasted dream,
Alone again, what did it mean?

Jennifer Marchant

OLD AGE

In the park they sit
Thoughts of the past years
Hampered by their failing wit
Their eyes filling with tears

With their young ones long gone
And ample time to think and ponder
Always seem to hum the same song
Isn't it time for a little wonder

Tea is near, that's it for today
Cup in one hand, paper in other
Trying to read what they really say
They're all wrong, so what's the bother?

Then off to bed to rest and think
What should be done to youth of today
Most of them have long hair and stink
This is not our problem to solve anyway.

Jim Potter

PAPER TO MONEY

It starts as a tree, then you do see
Large trunks of wood transported to the factory
It then gets treated and made to a pulp
After processing there is an end result
Paper, card, and money too
Without it what would we do?
Well money may buy you the things that you desire
And money will be handy when you retire.
You might be fortunate to have some wealth
But remember, money won't buy you health.
So share your fortune that you do hold
And give some happiness to the young and old.
Help people who are sick and in need
For today the world is full of greed.
You will feel much better in your heart
If only some of your fortune, you do part.
So share your good fortune with others too
And remember money, you can't take it with you.
As one day it will come to us all,
A wooden overcoat! And it won't matter if you're
Short, fat or tall!

V M Seaman

To You

So long ago, on windswept hill
In church I vowed and said 'I will.'
Our love displayed, no longer hid,
'Twas the best day's work I ever did.

We've travelled far, my darling wife,
Through times of joy and days of strife.
Yet through it all we're still together,
So shall it be for ever and ever.

I can't begin to enumerate
All that I owe, my dearest mate.
Through you, my son and grandchild too,
All this and more, are due to you.

You show your love each day by day,
By thought and deed, the things you say.
To comfort, hearten, in all you do,
You really mean this - 'I love you.'

The years slip by and take their toll,
Contented now, we share our goal.
Changed by age, yet young at heart,
Still enjoined by Cupid's dart.

So now my love, I celebrate
All that you are, so good, so great,
Oh dearest one, my love still burns,
Have a wonderful day – many happy returns.

Maurice Bailey

HOSPITAL LIFE

My visit to the ward today
    Came to me in the strangest way
On seeing for once, the frail, sick and old.
    Cared and tended by nurses bold.
Each nurse so pretty, so clean and so gay
    Talking to patients in such a kind way.
Each one tended in an individual way
    Because of their frailties and sickness with age,
Whatever their feelings to those all around
    So, they were each comforted by nurses around.
So at the close of the day and the nurses away,
    They each had been comforted in some different way.
To look forward once more to the very next day
        or
To the nurses who help again in the very same way
Brightened by nurses young and gay.

Thelma Jean Cossham Everett

LIFE TODAY

The rush, the bustle
Maddening crowds
Busy shoppers,
Pubs so loud!

No time to speak
To passers by.
Empty smiles, and sadden faces
Looks of despair
An empty gaze.

If only we could slow our pace
Give time for thought,
And calm reflection

A difference then we would really see
A bonus in our life today!

Anne Hyde

LANGUAGE OF TONGUES

To give pain and hate,
Can only relate,
To those who find no love,
And this is a state,
For those who are jealous,
And even rebellious!
To one who has more,
And this is just jealous!
Don't confuse irritation,
To those without station,
As low is as high,
Can cause such creation,
They spy as they buy,
In the nearest found shop,
It's those happy spendthrifts,
Where gossip is bought.

Angela Helen

A Cry From The Wilderness

The forest cries out protect us from the rain that falls from the sky
The acid it contains is lethal, and eventually we die

The oceans wail protect us from the stupidity of man
He fills us with his rubbish, halting nature's plan

The skies call down protect us from poisonous CFCs
Which are contained in electrical goods, used by you and me

The river babbles protect me from the nitrates humanity dumps in
Thereby killing all the plants and fish which quietly live within

The animals shout protect us from cruel experiments
The ivory in the jewellery on which your money's spent

The jungles shout protect us from the raging saw
All in the name of industry now stripping the landscape raw

All that lives upon this earth is treated with contempt
Irrevocable damage has been done, and money can't be spent

But if man called out protect us, who will hear our call
Through all our selfish actions we have killed them all

How precious is our world to you
And is our aid too late?
Correct the problems that occur, internationally
Through man's greed and hate.

Lynda Fordham

INSPIRATION

Inspiration will come to you
When you need it most
It will even come to you
Whilst eating cheese on toast.

Munch on every mouthful
Enjoy it while you can
Inspiration is with you
You're inspiration's sort of man.

Inspiration will make things work
Of that you can be quite sure
Inspiration will keep you going
When things are getting dour.

Let inspiration hit you
Right between the eyes
Seize it, hold it, encourage it
Before inspiration dies.

Roger Stevens

RIVER THAMES

It's as old as time itself, this river wild and wide
I've watched its ever changing moods since I was a child
Then we dug in the sand or paddled the hours away
Lazing and dreaming day after day
The stars reflect in it from the skies
Like precious gems or sparkling eyes.
We used to sit with our feet in the sand,
And dream of the future - the things we planned!
He always wanted to go to the moon,
A young boy's dream, and over too soon.
I remember the nights in '43
When the river was calm and still as can be.
In the moonlight the bombers used it like a road
And followed it to London, their bombs to unload
An old tea clipper I've seen sail by too,
With billowing sails and a singing crew.
And many years later we sat on the grass
And waited for hours to see Chichester pass
But it had no mercy in '53
When a raging storm lashed sea,
Burst its banks on the sleeping folk
And took its toll when the sea wall broke.
Then followed a night of fear and dread
When the tide receded we counted our dead.
After all these years the children still play
On the same old beach, in the same old way.
I expect the children still dream as we did then
Man has been to the moon, and back again.
The young man has been gone many years too
Not one of his dreams did ever come true.
The people are different but the river's the same,
Lapping and slapping – grey and untamed.

Dorothy Bond

THOUGHTS OF LOVE

As Christmas time is drawing near
These thoughts of love I want you to hear
For the love of my mother I've written some lines
In memory of some of our happier times
I'll never forget our days together
We laughed and cried in all sorts of weather
Shopping on Saturdays would take all day
But home again we would make our way
We'd then relax for a moment or two
With a cup of tea and time to review
All we had bought and the fun we'd had
Returning home penniless, but very glad
How I wish those days were here again –
I wouldn't be writing this sad refrain

Janet (Tuthill) Carter

My Dad: Albert Edward Booth

I want to remember my ole man
As I knew him years ago
Albert was a gentleman
Carrying weights and barbells in his show
Albert joined the army
And he learned how to kill!
He sent Hitler barmy
And put the Jerries on the pill
My dad, he liked his football
And anything on TV:
And anything with a ball
Until they lost it in a tree
My dad, he'd like a drink
And in his ole old days
It helped him kinda think
He'd maybe win the lottery
Now my ole man's gone
Well Dad, you won't be forgotten
In my eyes you didn't do a thing wrong
We're all missing you and I feel rotten.

Winston Bryan

WONDERFUL LIFE

Wonder at everything, bubbles, flowers, rain
Wonder about the triumphs, the losses, the pain

Wonder about the adventure of being alive
Wonder leads to magic, awe and surprise

Wonder about how the story will unfold
Live a life of wonder, where the end is untold

Wonder with curiosity like a small child
With wonder life is natural, earthly and wild

Hoping is struggle, like a swimmer against the tide
Wonder is easy, like a drifting boat at the lakeside

No expectations, just wonder
No attachments, just wonder

Wonder is the ultimate freedom

Andrea Darling

PUTTING THE CLOCKS BACK

I hate it when the clocks go back
And people start to sneeze and hack.
Then summer seems so far away
When there's so little light for play.

Every morning the car is damp
Dimly lit by an orange street lamp.
Then I hear on the radio
There's forty shopping days to go.

Approaching Christmas, I'll ascend
A hill of cards that I must send,
And drag around the crowded stores,
Purchasing, while my spending soars.

But when I reach the shortest day
I'll know that light is on the way.

Ann Nunan

SMILES

Universal smile of love, heaven's heart, the golden dove,

Pleasures riches warm embrace,
Fuels the touch of the arms of grace,
The polish the face with its shine inspired,
Flame friendship fruitful foundation fired,

Smile grow to laughter, happiness blooms,
Spread the smile and bliss its aisle, to style to groom,
Warmth of spirit from within,
A beam that glows, like the joys of spring.

The eyes that flow with goodness,
A smile so warm and free,
Lights the spirit of inspiration,
A friend and good company.

The soul that lives with goodness gives,
Refreshing sips of life to live,
The lines of time look with style,
Younger each day to live with a smile.

D A Davies

I LEARNT MY LESSON

Driving lessons between husband and wife
Are the biggest causes of marital strife
He sits on the edge of the passenger seat
Poised for escape and a hasty retreat
He fidgets and twitches as if he's got fleas
Pale of face and clutching his knees
After less than an hour he starts to shout
On that note, I usually get out!

The first test I didn't pass
Two men crossed the road with a sheet of glass
Looking at them gave me a fright
I completely missed the red traffic light!

The second test I'd rather not mention
Driving without due care and attention
The third one was fair, almost there
Reversing a corner I had to swerve
Avoiding a dog, I hit the curb
After that I lost my nerve.

Several years later, a new location
A fourth test taken with trepidation
This time I passed - what jubilation!
Still married too - what celebration!

Pamela Porter

TIDDLES

Tiddles, the cat strolled out at dark
Bristled with fear, when hearing a bark
Dreams were shattered, what could he do?
Nothing at all, he needed the loo.

Daisy Cooper

CLASS ACT

Into the classroom and on to the floor,
Our teacher, Miss Rimmer, danced in through the door.
She taught us a song by a man she called Frank,
Then marched us to assembly, soldiers in rank.
We all sang some songs and we prayed to God,
And assembly was finished with a smile and a nod.
Back in the classroom, we went on a trip –
An actor. A winger, in full England strip.
A doctor, a pilot, a cowboy, a clown;
We opened our books and we wrote it all down.
Out on the playground, Daniel was sick,
And David chased Anthony with a big stick.
Back to our counting in twos, fives and tens,
Right up to one hundred and back again!
We sang about numbers and days of the week.
We wrote them on whiteboards with pens that went squeak.
Dinner was yummy. Pizza and chips!
I ate it all up, smacking my lips.
We sailed on the Nile to a land called Egypt,
With pyramids and camels and a Pharaoh's crypt.
We read hieroglyphics and then wrote some words
With squiggles and shapes and people and birds.
I played in the sandpit with Ann Marie Bright,
We built us a castle with a king and a knight.
We went to the Lego and built a great town,
Then time for a story, Miss sat us all down.
She told us of dragons, a king and a queen
And the prettiest princess you've ever seen.
Then out of the classroom to mum's velvet touch,
She asks what I've done. I shrug, 'Nothing much!'

Joanne Cross

FOR MY BELOVED MOTHER
WHO HAS ALZHEIMER'S DISEASE

I've known this lady all my life.
She was there at the beginning.
I hold her hand, with my heart in it and my head spinning.
She can't remember who I am.
Her eyes are cloudy and dim.
But when I call her mother, she smiles a toothless grin,
I could be anyone.
I tell her all my bits of news,
Her mind is a total blank.
She tries so hard to understand the balance in her bank.
The anger is there,
The pain, frustration and rage.
Trapped inside a body that's riddled with old age.
She was once a nursing sister,
She can't remember that -
Nor the time Aunt Jane sat on the chair and flattened her best hat.
She sits unmoving day by day.
The hand I hold a claw,
Her wrinkled face smiles goodbye, as I go out the door.
Mum doesn't know that I have been, or what day is today.
She doesn't even know her name, or how she came this way.
Yesterday does not exist, there may not be tomorrow.
Today drags on with heavy heart and eyes just full of sorrow.

Sandi Cooper

MY PAL

I was feeling quite down
This morning
Inwardly moaning my lot
When all of a sudden
My phone rang,
You called and my downs were forgot.
You lifted my spirits
You gave me a laugh.
You told me a fresh tale or two.
I thank God at the end of the day
I have a good friend
And it's you!
We are always there for each other
Whatever the problem may be.
We can talk about anything
On our minds.
It will remain between you and me.
We know we can always trust one another,
Whatever we have to say.
That is what friendship is all about,
Sharing and caring - in every way.

Molly Ann Kean

BRITANNIA

Britannia weeps for her sons once so proud
Who kept these isles free from forces outside
Now they give Britain and all she holds dear
To the Common Market countries who give a loud cheer

They could not get her with bombs or guns
They tried their hardest, those grim-faced Huns
The French gave in quickly to the German threat
Relied on Britain to sort out the mess

This small island for hundreds of years
Has fought on bravely through blood and tears
We did not need help to keep the flag flying
Why give in now, this country's not dying
Cling to your rights, keep Britain free
We don't need to join any Community

Violet Gray

FRIENDSHIP

The knowledge that a person cares just what you say and do;
That all the things you love so well, they think a lot of, too.
A feeling of respect and trust for one whom you admire,
Who helps you when you're worried, and never seems to tire.

The feeling that they always share when life seems far from kind
Relying on their sympathy when something's on your mind.
The one who always understands just what you really mean,
Who never tries to pry into the things you don't want seen.

The knowledge that they're happy when good fortune comes your way;
And, far from feeling jealous, try to make life still more gay.
Who knows just when you're lonely, and you're needing company,
And yet who leaves you when it's plain, alone you'd rather be.

Who compliments you, (when deserved) without a fuss or show;
Whose tact you can rely on, when your pride has had a blow.
And yet who always airs his views when prejudiced you seem,
Suggesting mild deflation, when puffed up with self-esteem!

All these and many other things my friendship with you means -
And so I hope I'll always hold it through life's changing scenes.

J Packwood

WEATHER

What a load of old rubbish it's too cold.
I can't stand this, it's just not hot.
Braving the weather is an act so bold,
If I could afford it, I'd go abroad like a shot.

For our special two weeks away
More than one hot day in a row.
Great memories of that sunny stay
Baking slowly to gain that all round glow.

Andrew Crump

THE SUBMARINE

Barnacles over and under the grey submarine
rising above sparkling white sand
of the shimmering rocky beach.
Boy, accompanied by large cross-breed dog,
race toward their make-believe land.

A rising sea sweeps about their vessel,
not yet sufficient to prevent them boarding her.
'Make haste! Make haste, Mr Mate!' the captain cries,
as with a mighty leap the dog reaches the deck.
Salutes his captain saying, 'That was close sir.'

Frothing sea swirls about the submarine
scouring a deep channel around the hull.
Dog and boy challenge the rushing tide,
dashing from deck to shore and back again.
Laughing at the inquiring cry of the gulls.

Six feet of the two contented mariners
plod wearily homeward as the sun sinks low.
Their voyage successful despite dangers
from sirens, mermaids and other sprites.
The sun and wind bring faces aglow.

Robert Allen

PAIN

I met the woman of my dreams
Not so long ago,
For she was perfect,
And I loved her so.
There's nothing she wouldn't do for me
And she loved me just as much,
We both fell in love together,
And yearned each other's touch.
In time we both got married,
And lived in wedded bliss.
There was nothing that could part us,
Even when we'd kiss.
For I had met my soulmate,
And for nothing I did want.
So for this I called her Angel,
And walked her to the font.
For this was the woman I'd waited for,
For all my life long days,
My God-sent angel from above,
And I loved her ways.
She showed me what a true love meant,
So all our days together spent,
This woman was my angel,
And from Heaven sent.
Then for some unknown reason,
My angel changed her ways,
No longer did she love me
Or with me would she stay.
My heart now it is aching,
My body it is numb,
For I have lost my angel,
And my life has come undone.
Now I live in darkness,

My angel's gone away,
And I won't love another,
Until my dying day.
For when you've loved an angel,
No other can compare,
And if you meet that angel
Treat with tender care,
Because if you do not,
You'll suffer pain, beyond repair!

Steffan AP Lloyd

JUST WORDS

so many things I want to say
it's the way I start, I begin each day

from my morning coffee
to my afternoon tea

nothing but words
spill out of me

words like explanation
and words I don't know

it's all I can do
to go with the flow

when will they stop
I really don't know?

And when they do
where will they go?

Will they go
to some unfortunate soul?

Just like me
like I was before

but if you ask
I'm not really complaining

because I'll be sad
when these words, they stop raining

Andrew Hunter

WHAT IS LIFE?

What is life? Life is a breath of
spring air in a day or a week or year.
You can see it go by with the
blinking of an eye
Life is for loving and giving and making a living,
A companion is life through four score and ten.
It's seen in different ways in many countries and fen.
So precious is life it's like taking
a wife one minute all lightness
and flowers.
Some may nag you by the hour.
When a young breeze blows through
it's not for me, it's not for you
to reason what life's about.
But it's good to be alive, so shout it out.

Raymond Law

MY BOOK

A book upon my shelf proclaims
600 town and country names
From Abbotsford to Zennor fair
The biggest and the best are there

And in the twilight of my room
I long to own a magic broom
To carry me to unseen places
Gentle folk with smiling faces

I'll need no one to be my guide
Upon my broomstick I will ride
To sample Britain's sweet delights
Midst travelled days and restful nights

Through Ashby-de-la-Zouch I'll fly
In summer breeze and cloudless sky
Proud Penzance will appeal to me
With lofty cliffs and crashing sea

Through Flint and Fleet and Felixstowe
Midst autumn gales and winter snow
I'll fly my broomstick everywhere
Without a worry or a care

And when my flying days are through
I'll pass my book of names to you
That you may choose with boundless grace
Our last together nesting place

Dennis Bensley

SONG OF A TRAVELLING MAN

One day down on the
Double-decker lay-by
Clicker rocker roadway
Clicker rocker road!

Shimmer gimmer gim-sham
Wheeling up the Jim Jam
Shammer jammer freeway
Just another load!

One night up on the
Whirly-girly road race
Hurly-burly gold chase
Never-ever stop!

Ribber dibber old van
Clacking on the autobahn,
Reeling keeling life span
Travel till you drop!

Patricia Crouter

LIFE IS REALITY

Maybe we have to live the words we write,
Feel in our hearts the strings so tight.
Shed the tears, just let them flow.
As on our road of life we go.
Meetings, greetings, togetherness,
Then perhaps two lives shared . . . no less.

But life may not be that way,
Other forces may hold sway . . . win the day.
Hearts and feelings mix and match
Entwine, unite, and then detach.

You must not despair. Pause awhile, this is a stile . . .
To climb. Look around. What outlets can be found?
Setbacks challenge our ability to cope -
While we breathe, we hope.
Determined we must be, life is reality, so . . .
Head high. the road may be long.
Just carry on, be strong, seize the opportunity -
To make your dream of life . . . a reality.

D L Huff

TERROR

Terror rises around the globe
wearing its bloodstained robe
crippling the souls of its actors
destroying all moral factors

The Devil's distorted face
crushed clear conscience and its base
tears all feelings from human hearts
turns the globe into splintered parts

Terror takes its sadistic gallop
races along without halt nor stop
like a black horse without any reins
crosses all borders, leaving crude pains

Even in front of an abyss on its way
it may overleap it and cause dismay
its race may go on for centuries ahead
if by hate and corruption it is fed

Terror conquers the human mind
its remedy will no one find
unless a dove of love will seek
and retrieve an olive twig in its beak

Wila Yagel

HENMANIA

The angry sky reflects the mood of the tennis player
As he packs his bags again

The disgruntled crowd shelter beneath a shower
Of multicoloured umbrellas as the rain
Pours down.

Aspirations drown.

The champion retains his crown. For now!
But tomorrow is another day.

Weather permitting.

Ben Wolfe

THE TREE HOUSE

Andrea rushed into the kitchen 'Mum, come quick and see,
It's Dad, he's making a tree house, he's hammering nails in your
favourite tree.'
'Don't worry, I know what I'm doing. I loved playing trees as a lad,
I'll just nail in this platform for Claira, it will be her very own
special pad,'
'Please don't put in more nails Chris, I really like this tree.'
'Don't worry, I know what I'm doing, Claira will love it, just see.'
Claira handed the nails to Taid, he made the platform secure.
'Climb up now Claira and try it, you'll love it, of that I'm sure.'
Claira was very excited, Lucy stood watching with glee.
'I wish I was big like Claira, I want to sit up in that tree.'
Harriet scrambled around in a frenzy . . . 'I wish I could climb that tree
I wish I was big like Claira, but I'm sure Claira will help me . . . '
'Taid, it's too high for Lucy and Harriet and I'd like them up here with
me. Could you make some steps for them Taid, *Please!* to help them
climb into my tree?'
Taid got some more wood from the garage, he got his hammer and nails
out too. 'If it's steps that you need, don't worry, I'll make them
specially for you.' Three steps Taid nailed into the tree, Nain was now
getting upset.
'No more nails, please, enough is enough!'
'Oh, I've finished, don't worry, don't fret.'
By now Lucy and Harriet were tired, they toddled off elsewhere to play,
But Claira climbed up in her tree house, to enjoy the rest of the day.
'Thanks Taid, you're so clever.' Job finished Taid relaxed in the sun.
But his peace was very soon shattered. Claira wanted just wanted
more fun. 'Taid I could do with a rope ladder,'
'Claira I could do with a rest.'
'Oh! but Taid you make such good things.'
Taid's patience was put to the test.
After much pulling and tugging, a rope ladder was made and secured.
So Claira at last had her tree house, and at last Taid's peace
was restored.

Frances Roberts

GLOBAL PEACE

Since my birth in '42
Many things happened in my life
Some are wonderful memories
Others were troubles and strife.

First came the end of WWII
Then Korea and Vietnam
The Suez Canal and Falkland Isles
Kuwait and Afghanistan.

There will always be the trouble spots
In Asia, China or Taiwan
Where loss of life fighting for peace
Will be in a foreign land.

Many soldiers and civilians have died
Inside those battle zones
They died for liberation and peace
And the defending of their homes.

I wish for a global peace
To live and be as one
And live together in harmony
Until life on Earth has gone.

John Gwynne

LIKE AN EAGLE

My son has golden locks so fair
A Rastafarian style of hair
But now it's gone and left a sheen
And all his bumps and lumps are seen!

For with that mode of hair you see
He can't become an employee
For bosses look for outward show
A suit, a tie, a dickey bow!

And now see what they've gone and done
Fought a battle hard and won!
As if such tresses were illegal
My son now favours the bald-eagle!

But whatever pattern takes his hair
Whatever clothes he opts to wear
He's still my one and only son
I love him, when all's said and done!

Trish Duxbury

TREE OF LIFE

A song without a melody.
Who's afraid, me or thee?
A shallow heart, a stony view
Our future is a mere review,
Of all the sorrow and the pain
From all the possessions that we gain
Mother Nature here she cries
As she looks through human eyes.
Self destruction is our game.
When will we learn that all the gifts
Are here to take.
Whenever we learn to awake?

Carol Bairstow

A SCHOOLBOY ALONE

I'm a little schoolboy,
I can't stand the school.
People keep on hurting me,
They are being cruel.

I try to take no notice,
But they keep hurting more.
I don't like the teachers,
Friends, I've none at all.

I ran away from school one day,
The teacher brought me back,
The children then would pick on me,
But I would not hit back.

Day after day it's always the same,
You try to tell the teachers,
But they don't make a change.
I say the children's parents are the ones to blame.

The children beat me up,
They still call me names,
I still hate this school,
The fact I have no friends at this dreaded school.

Tony Grierson

NEW YORK, NEW YORK

The immortal words New York, New York
Always ring throughout my thoughts
A city thousands of miles away
It's always thought about during my day

Where steam blows through hot pavement slabs
Where the concrete jungle rules to the last
Glittering streets whisper secrets to me
About the inhabitants of this great city

What can I say about this place?
It never sleeps; it's neither night nor day
Relax in Central Park or go up the Empire
'It's the closest thing to Heaven,' as she says with a smile

Blocks upon blocks of streets look and stare
Reminds me of times past unseen and unaware
Looking over the city the calmness takes effect
For the city stops, lights glimmer, flicker and glare.

N Wright

TAGS

There is a man on the street,
whose eyes people will not meet.
He holds forth a magazine,
an emblem of all he is or has been.
It shouts homeless, worthless, pity me
and that is all the passers-by ever see;
of a person faceted as a bright-cut gem.
The blinkers are firmly set on them.
But each in turn is labelled
by their own array of markers cabled together -
a car, carrier bags, even clothes,
are they worth knowing? Judge by those.
But who lies behind them, what's at the core
is anyone certain anymore?

Nicola Grant

TEN GREEN POEMS

Ten green poems I'm able to recall,
Ten graffiti items, fairly off the wall.
And if one green poem should not appeal to all,
There'll be nine green poems still sprayed upon the wall.

Nine green heroes standing straight and tall,
Nine clean heroes, skilled with bat and ball.
And if one keen hero, discredited, should fall,
There'll be eight clean heroes still to please us all.

Eight green species clinging to the wall,
Eight green species climbing up the wall,
And if one green boffin should modify them all,
There'll be seven shades of colour displayed upon the wall.

Seven shades of viewpoint debated in the hall,
Seven shades of viewpoint created in the hall,
But if one strong opinion should over-ride them all,
There'll be six minds to wither like flowers in the fall.

Six rare specimens standing in a stall,
Six rare specimens standing in a stall.
But, far from Mother Nature, they've forgotten how to crawl.
There'll be five rare specimens and one we can't recall.

Five keen senses were given to us all,
Five keen senses at our beck and call,
But if we never hearken to the voices still and small,
There'll be four lost listeners we never knew at all.

Four lost listeners stranded in the throng,
Four lost listeners tried to get along.
There was one lost listener who found another song,
Leaving three lost listeners stranded in the throng.

Three lost prisoners trapped behind the gate.
Three lost prisoners, is it merely fate?
Take a chance and let one out, kindly re-instate.
For two lost prisoners will it be too late?

Two lost pensioners, maybe one is you.
Two lost pensioners hadn't got a clue.
One approached the internet, found out what to do.
There was one last pensioner standing in the queue.

One poetic pensioner scribbled now and then.
This poetic pensioner soon mislaid his pen.
Hedged around by happenings quite beyond my ken,
I got myself arrested when I sprayed the wall again!

No green sentiments sprayed upon the wall,
No furry animals cuddlesome and small,
No youth, no joy, no happiness, no kisses in the hall.
Too late to come a'looking when there's nothing left at all.

John Guy

THE LOST HRT PATCH

I've lost me HRT patch, I don't know where it went
I do know I'm so anxious the time that I have spent
To search the likely places it may have become detached
I'm running out of places now my anxiety's unmatched
I've tried the obvious places like pants, bath and nightie
But so far come up with nothing, it is a task almighty
I had it on the Thursday, I'm not sure at what time
Come Friday I'm beside myself, it almost seems a crime
I've watched both cat and dog in case their behaviour's erratic
But so far they're quite normal, why do I feel so frantic
One reason could be I suppose the purpose that I have them
Is to calm the moods and flushes down and decorate me bum.

Marion Jones

OH! MEN OF SCIENCE! - AND CHIPS

'The time has come,' Professor said,
'To talk of micro-chips;
Of circuitry and gadgetry;
Come, let us get to grips
With talk of hardware, software too;
Computers large and small;
And laser beams and other rays;
Of physics overall.'

I know these things are mental food
And mental drink as well,
To learned men like you and him,
But, hold hard. Can't you tell,
When lowlier folk go 'glassy-eyed'
And open fall their lips,
It's time to cut the learned stuff
And talk of *fish* and chips!

C A L Bairstow

I'M BORED

I'm bored, I'm *really* bored
I got up this morning and looked through the windowpane
And yes, of course, you've guessed it, it was pouring down with rain
Another day to stay indoors, wondering what to do
I know, I'll make a cup of tea, just wait for it to brew

I'm bored, I'm *really* bored
I'd read another book, but I know they've all been read
I'd sort out all my houseplants,
But I forgot to water them so they're dead
I would do some knitting, but my wool has all run out
I'd even do some sewing, but there's no material about.

I'm bored, I'm *really* bored
I could watch the telly, but I've seen it all before
No one comes to see me, no one knocks upon my door
I can't phone anybody, I can't afford it anymore
I'd write to someone, but I've already written four

I'm bored, I'm *really* bored
Hey, that's funny, it's gone dark outside, what time can it be?
It's ten o'clock at night, oh dear, oh dear, dear me
It just shows that it's true, what I have always said
Time flies when you enjoy yourself, so now I'm late for bed!

Sylvia Derbyshire

BLACKBERRY JAM AND SLOE GIN

Across the field, leaving river behind,
to sloping woods where we will find
blackberries and sloes to pick,
but watch out for the brambles' prick.
Trees and bushes all overrun
craning upwards to face the sun.
Here the best fruit can be found
ripening high above the ground.
Stretch up over many a thorn
sleeves and jumpers soon are torn.
The prize, plump berries to gather in
for our blackberry jam and sweet sloe gin.

Gerard Chamberlain

DREAMTIME

The Aborigine's believe this,
It's a part of their ways,
It's seen in their paintings
Listen to what it says.

If I had a dreamtime
I'd wish the world well,
Fill it full of laughter
Colourful stories I would tell.

Take care of our planet
Before it turns on us.
People say that's crazy
What is all the fuss?

But whatever your religion
Take heed, your god will come
To repay for all wrong doing
Forgiving only some.

Let us join together
In unity through and through.
Don't forget your brothers
Those you hardly knew.

In one flash of lightning
A thunderbolt will strike
Wiping out thousands
Even those you like.

If I had the power
I'd turn off the lights
Take out all the bad bits
And soar to amazing heights.

Meryl Stacey Hulber

TRIP TO THE FARNE ISLANDS

On Sunday, we went to the Farnes
And saw a host of birds flying.
Some were mean, others were good
And some on their nests were lying.

We saw hundreds of cormorants
Nesting, with their young
Perched on a rock, perched on a ledge,
Squawking and showing their tongue.

There were many colonies of kittiwakes
Flying overhead,
Looking for food, in the calm sea.
Soon, more fish would be dead.

X-shaped guillemots racing
This way and that past our boat.
On the sea puffins, eiders too
All managing to stay afloat.

We landed on Inner Farne,
Where terns were defending their eggs.
They dived to attack everyone there,
Pecking at heads and bare legs.

There were puffins all over the place;
Rainbow bills and bright orange feet.
Flying to burrows, beaks flashing silver-
Fish for their babies to eat.

All too soon it was time to go home
And face vicious terns once more,
Say goodbye to the shags, the fulmars and gulls.
I'll be back one day, though, for sure.

Timothy Jasper

CHRISTMAS

Christmas is the time,
When you think of me the most,
When you wish that you could see,
A tiny glimpse of me.

You know that I live on,
So why are you so sad?
When really you should be kind of glad,
For I am with you everyday,
Whatever you may say.

'I'll be there watching over you.'

Please don't cry for me,
'Cause we'll have a cup of tea,
When it's your time,
To head for the light,
I will be there just out of your sight.

The door will be opened,
It's just up to you,
Whether or not you want to pass through.

There will be family and friends,
All there at your send off,
So don't be afraid to pass over,
We'll all go and visit the White Cliffs of Dover.

Red Hawk Through Mathew Spry

UNTITLED

I watch the day distance itself over
Hampstead Heath and from an open window
Of a psychiatric ward I wonder
With the last steadfast leaves falling below
Why am I here? Were the nights as a child
With my mother and our endless journey
Through the streets of Leeds, through desperate wild
Rain just to end in vain in a room here?
While November trees hold the listless leaves
Held within the first fold of memory,
How the end of a single leaf retrieves
The meaning I have lost, how childhood's key
Is broken fast within its lock. Leaves late
In their own stillness falter as I wait.

Brenda Williams

WHAT ONE BULLET DID

Remember, remember the 5th of November,
Of gunpowder, treason and plot.
Remember, remember the 11th of November,
It's somewhere that we were not.
The Great War was the real beginning,
Of the depravation of all mankind.
Mustard gas and muddy shellholes,
Brought to life's end a lot of blokes.
Sieges of wipers gate there were,
Many, until the fields were bare.
Jutland's seas saw England's line of battle,
Jolly jack tars tripping over tackle.
Kaiser's ships they turned at bay,
Smoke and flame, oh, such a fray,
Till at last stalemate was called,
Huns no food to fill them all.
Peace was signed in a railway coach,
People thought it was a hoax.
Guns fell silent, peace in the air,
Huns and Tommies left their lairs.
Returning at last to families and home,
Each man returned and found lots gone.
Jobs galore when you found the work,
Until the day that Wall Street fell.
Depression came, starvation too,
Till greed and envy took their toll.

Kenneth Copley

THE RELUCTANT ASTRONAUT

Nosey Parker, Aggie Shannon looked down the business
                              end of a cannon.
The cannon popped and so did she and no one's seen her since but me
And that is why I now relate her very sad and awful fate.
That well-remembered afternoon she took off heading for the moon.
And soon she made her presence felt as she crashed
                              through the asteroid belt
Ripping some asteroids right in two as six-foot Ag went racing through.
She pushed a comet out in space careering on her zany race
And as she was about to swoon she took a header for the moon.
She landed safely on her face and thought this is a tasty place
Completely meets with all my favour, I do declare I like the flavour.
This mud would make a chocolate pud. It tastes so very
                              sweet and good.
A squelch as she pulled out her face attracted men from every place,
And as she raised her sticky dial they gave her just a sickly smile.
One moon man asked, 'Are you from Mars or have you
                              come from other stars?
We don't allow folks such as you to come here, this is what we do.'
They seized her by her legs and arms ignoring her attractive charms,
They put her on an elevator that let her down into a crater.
Then split an atom in her face and she went soaring into space.
And now she twinkles night and day, a new star in the Milky Way.

Margaret B Baguley

THE DANGER OF EATING MINT IMPERIALS
(While driving at eighty miles per hour in the outside lane of the M6
motorway in heavy traffic approaching The Knutsford Service Station)

High
speed
mouth
feed.

Mint
suck,
good
luck.

Get
bored
Knuts
ford.

Gulp,
cough,
swerve
off.

Large
van.
Oh!
damn!

Smash,
crash,
help
dash.

Tough,
mate,
too
late.

David W Lankshear

THE HEADACHE

Father has a headache,
He's sprawling in the chair,
He wears a pained expression -
Mum is tearing out her hair!

He winces with each little noise,
He moans at every sound,
He sighs about each whispered word -
Mum is tiptoeing around.

He is dying for some aspirin,
He needs a glass of water,
An ice pack would be soothing -
Mum's fuse is getting shorter.

What's that? There's football on the telly!
He'll just check out the score,
Mum's mutter of disapproval
Is lost in the crowd's great roar.

Father is watching the football
He fancies some tea and a beer,
But Mum has got a headache -
'Oh - just take an aspirin, dear!'

Ruth Cargill

A PRISON CELL

There's Emmy the thief,
Betty the pro'
Plus Evelyn, who's stabbed her beau,
Daft old Letty, who has no teeth,
Ida, who's laid out fast asleep,
Then there's me, I've done no wrong,
I got locked up, for singing a song,
Out there my friends asked me to sing,
They always do when I've had some gin,
I love to sing, when I've had my drink,
But not singing now, I'm in the clink,
A boy screams out, at the sound of the cat,
Ten heavy lashes across his bare back,
Oh, I hope I will not be forgotten,
It's cold in here, and stinks so rotten,
When Mammy knows, she'll bail me out,
Accompanied by a great big clout!

Kathleen Biesiekirski

AGE CONCERN

I've read in books
About old people's looks
That their ears and their nose
Still grows!
Now the ears grow so
That the hearing won't go
But it does go you know
So it just can't be so.
Now a nose that starts small
Won't change much at all
But a nose that starts longer
Leaves something to ponder.
If it just grows and grows
Would it soon reach the toes
And if the old back is bent
And the nose still has scent
That again gives something to ponder,
With a nose growing yonder and yonder.
Long ears you can hide
In a nice woolly hat!
But a mile-a-minute nose
What's to do about that!
A hanging basket sounds fine
With pretty flowers and vine
And as it reaches the feet
Would keep the feet sweet
'Til they close down the casket
Then the preacher can relate
She made a great hanging-basket
But was a martyr to her fate.

Constance I Roper

POLE AXED

No need to reproach, said the national team coach,
to the national pole vaulting team,
the pole I supplied, wouldn't allow you to glide,
to the heights of a pole vaulter's dream.

The mix up began, when our relay team ran,
and the record we broke by one minute,
but the baton we held, was as long as when felled,
and the judge said that's no way to win it.

The message sank in, as the coach stroked his chin,
and thought the whole thing can't all be my fault,
you've seen poles before, in the national team store,
so remember the next time you vault.

Did you not know the score, when your chins scraped the floor,
that the pole was much shorter than usual,
with your legs all akimbo, it looked like the limbo
a horse would have made a refusal.

But don't get upset, we'll all triumph yet,
when next time we enter the games,
we'll place a big bet, on our pole vaulting set,
and Guinness will know all our names.

But next time they competed, they all were defeated,
and the javelin team were also downhearted
cos the spears they threw, somehow went askew,
and the vaulters were back where they started.

Thomas B McDonald

SHOCKING SHOPPING

Granddaughter took her granny out shopping,
But, Grandmother thought her shopping was shocking
She wanted some 'frillies' and other bits too.
But when she bought panties her grandmother spued.
They were frilly and dainty and also see through -
Now Grandmother said, 'Now, they will not do!'
'Oh Grandma,' she said, 'you're right out of date,
No wonder my grandad plays music so late!'

J Mary Kirkland

I AM LOVED AS I AM

I may not be who you want me to be
I may not see the things you see
but am I really that different? Do you think I am strange?
Is there a part of me you would like to change?

Stop for a minute, don't be in such a haste
rushing around like you have no time to waste.
There really is not that much difference between you and I
we all have faults, cover them up though we try.

But wait, maybe there is a slight difference.
What? You ask - what can it be?
Well, when you look in the mirror what do you see?

Because when I look I see eyes full of love and a heart full of joy
secure in God's love which no one can take away or destroy.
Look, can you see it, can you see what I do?
No, then turn away, turn towards, look again, see it now.
Yes, He loves you too.

Gladys Lawson

WILDLIFE TALES OF HYLTON CASTLE - OUTFOXING THE FOX

From Hylton Castle woods, the rabbits fled pell mell
Raynard the fox was around, and giving them hell,
Up to the hill overlooking Hylton Castle they ran,
Fearing Raynard the fox, more than any mere man,
In the woods, they had played hopping about,
When the cry, 'The fox! The fox is about!' was the shout.

Nearing the hill, Sid skunk they did see,
He always visited them on Sundays for tea,
'Why my friend,' he asked, 'what is it that frightens thee?'
'Raynard the fox,' one baby rabbit cried, 'he's chasing me.'
'Right,' Sid said, 'to your burrow with you I will go,
For many a kindness from you, many a favour I owe.'

Deep in their burrows the rabbits cowered in fear,
Knowing fine well, soon Raynard the fox would be here,
At the entrance to the burrow, Sid stood his ground,
Standing on guard, he made no sound,
Up the hill Raynard ran with all speed,
A nice juicy rabbit, he thought, that's what I need,

At the burrow entrance, be began to scramble and dig,
Hoping that the first rabbit he caught would be big,
Sid skunk with a snout, his smell he gave out,
From the burrow it oozed, into Raynard's big mouth,
The fox stopped digging in startled surprise,
Coughing and spluttering, the tears ran from his eyes,

Down the River Wear, Raynard now made his way,
Catching a rabbit for him would have to wait another day,
Into the water he went with full speed,
He knew that a wash was what he did need,
Going home to his wife, covered in the smell of skunk,
Could well cause his vixen to do a bunk.

R Marr

THE TIGHTROPE WALKER

The girl lay sobbing at his feet
The man he lay there dying
'Come on my girl,' he softly said
'On your feet and stop your crying.'

That walk across the cliffs today
Was done just for a dare
No one had walked that way before
And the chance to do it was rare.

I got halfway across the rope
My heart was full of hope
And then the wind began to blow
The story now you know.

I fell down from quite a height
And hit the water with a splash
My friends were there on the other side
And after me they began to dash.

The river began to carry me
As my name again they called
I lay there in the water
As it carried me to the falls.

The current carried me over the top
And down the other side
A plume of spray arched right down
As through it I began to slide.

I hit my head upon a rock
And sank just like a stone
And as I drifted slowly up
I dreamt that I was not alone.

A voice spoke to me soft and slow
And others began to sing
As I listened to their song
A bell began to ring.

I asked for time to speak to you
To say farewell at last
The voice said that they would wait for me
For now my life is past.

The girl she took him in her arms
Her voice was full of dread
The words she spoke were heeded not
For the man in her arms - was dead.

Trevor Headley

BESTEST DREAM

(I dedicate this poem to Eileen Regan (course tutor of Counselling Skills) and those I met on this course)

Memories of the smiles left behind
What a simple message to give,
a message of liking and acceptance
'Thank you, I am glad I met you'
If a smile could speak that's what it would say
Memories of how we cared and shared,
of hearts that shined like a summer's day
We worked together like a team,
just like the bestest dream

Daniel White

THE INNER PEARL

How close she sat - this little girl
That sat so quiet - this precious pearl
Whose life had been confused and torn
Between two loves - a life forlorn
Of true stability, peace of mind
But in the shadows do I find
A mirror image - only smaller
My own reflection - which is taller

We sat and watched a children's play
I felt her move - what will she say?
She gave to me a kiss so warm
I felt the tears begin to form
Behind my eyes - oh! what a joy
To have this gift - and not a ploy
For any other means or gain
Love truly given - it was plain
To see what I had never heeded
Sat so close - I never needed
An outside judge to prove my worth
It was beside me here on Earth.

My dear grandchild - this darling girl
Is my reflection - my own true pearl
Of wisdom, worth and love divine
Was right within me all the time.

Gina Bowman

THE OLD CITY OF DURHAM

A Durham morning, cast in a grey winter's sky,
Where blows, harsh, very strong blustery winds,
See old streets that stand, in cobbled time,
Aged lanes lead the weary foot, and tired eyes.
Where once rode citizens, in carriages,
Pulled by horseshoed hoof,
Of maids in aprons and buckled shoes,
Served in markets scarce of stock, and paupers used.

In ale house, laughter and a fire's warming hearth,
Good men of Durham meet to drink and merrily laugh.
Jacobean beams, are set staid, into old house walls,
Within our time standing, but still ancient Durham calls.

In the old marketplace stands a weathered bronze statue -
This figure, a member of the Vane Tempest family,
Sitting still wearing his military uniform, in situ.
The Marquis of Londonderry, nobly seated on his bronze horse,
Watching along the marketplace's cobbled course.
Durham's streets are busy now with passing cars,
People stand, chat and shop to while away the hours.

The River Wear's water washes from the west,
Then round and through to course the east.
Round it washes, round this Holy Hill,
From the north it washes, rippled, never still.
Durham Cathedral staid, atop the trees, mightily above,
In refinement, and holiness, through times of ages stood.

The Bishop of Durham's throne, majestic stands high
To look down upon God's worshipping congregation,
From here the Right Reverent Michael Dunelm
Says prayers and blesses the queen's mighty nation.
Where priests preach sermons to mind the bad,
And there entombed lay, the saints, the good.

The ghosts of Benedictine monks, walk the priory halls,
Their chants and incantations can still be heard
Listen to where their voices, always to God, do call.
Where once rode Prince Bishop, and servant sage,
This city will stand to see, times futuristic change.

Susan Carole Gash-Roberts

BALLARD DOWN

Oh! To be on Ballard Down
By the ever restless tossing sea.
Where all the seagulls are crying
And the rage of the winds are blowing free.
As you walk on chalky grasses
It's a joyous place to hear the roar of the waves.
The sea birds are circulating in flashes
They appear to float on the water on a sunlit day.
Then, I gradually return to lower ground
And think of the beauty I have found.

Sammy Michael Davis

MARY

She bravely stood by Jeffrey's side,
What does she believe?
Her loyalty none can deride,
What do we believe?
'Not a penny more, not a penny less'
What does she believe?
'Twelve red herrings', maybe more,
What do we believe?
'Kane and Abel' to the fore,
What does she believe?
Is she blameless, is she pure?
What do we believe?
Not the 'Prodigal daughter' she
Though living in grand Grantchester,
Rupert Brooke's ghost softly whispers
'What do I believe?'
Her two sons, and Jeffrey's too,
What do they believe?
'A quiver full of arrows' fly
What do they believe?
Darling of the 'Blue rinse brigade',
What do they believe?
The runner, lover, author, speaker, MP,
Actor, playwright, statesman, liar! Thief!
Sure of himself, the great 'bouncer back'
Has at last come to grief!
All the prisoners in all the cells
Mutter aloud in their sad, long days
What do we believe?
What do we believe?
What does the world believe?
Only Jeffrey knows!
What does he believe?

V C Mary Hodson

REALISATION

A lifetime of memories
A fortress of dreams
Thoughts left unspoken
Forever it seems

So many feelings
Hidden away
Un-granted wishes . . .
But maybe, one day

I see through the window
A whisper of dew
An overcast morning -
The loneliest view

Fields lay in abundance
And gently unfold
The forgotten glory
And beauty they hold

Over distant hillsides
Through a sea of mist
Lay a carpet of heather
A picture of bliss

And just beyond
There's a rainbow, too
As the clouds break up
And the sun shines through

Unlock the windows
Of my mind
Once imprisoned
Now sublime

So here I am
Alone, but free
Now realising
What's meant to be

Everything seems beautiful
So natural, so divine
This moment is forever . . .
For these words will make it mine.

Pam Samways

VANITY

Oh God gift me with craft and brain
Till puffed up with pretension
And pray for me, the very vain.

I'll pass all tests, sing sweet refrain,
My every win make mention,
Oh God gift me with craft and brain.

I'll oft compete, ne'er lose again
A genius at invention,
And pray for me, the very vain.

Mensa I'll be, drive folk insane,
And revel in the tension.
Oh God gift me with craft and brain.

Deft dance ballet in Paris rain,
Swift sculpt with bold intention
And pray for me, the very vain.

Then all my works that cost no pain,
Will bring me fame and pension.
Oh God gift me with craft and brain,
And pray for me, the very vain.

Sarah Blackmore

IT'S ALWAYS WET!

It's going to be, cold, windy and wet!
So we're told, by the illustrious Met!
I'm sure they know that we will fret!
And put off washing day - I bet!
Not going out, just had my hair set!
And it's bound up in a net!
So I don't want to get it wet!
Should I pay a visit to a vet!
Wonder if he could find me a pet!
He may know one that can fetch, carry and get!
The things that I may need, from outside, when it's wet!
Because that is what we are in for, don't forget!
It's going to be cold, windy and wet!
So say the illustrious Met!
PS - Anyone going on their hols? Got a jet!

Joyce M Robinson

TEMPUS FUGIT

Time ticks on, as we all know,
As the hours and days quickly flow.
Whoever it was, who said 'How time flies!'
Was a person, extremely wise.

Weeks, then months, so soon have gone,
But, with luck, we carry on.
Schooldays flash by, as we know,
Then, into the wide world, we all go.

Soon decades have quickly sped away
And life goes on, day by day.
Then, like a bolt, out of the blue,
Your retirement day is nearly due!

Birthday's coming round, like a revolving door,
And I hope to see quite a few more.
But, the next one that I shall see
Is on July 30th when I will reach '80'.

Eddie Lawrence

WHO NEEDS A CAR?

I dream of a life without a car
I don't need to travel or go very far
All I need is my mobile to keep me in touch
To press the right buttons, it doesn't take much
To order some food, life is a song
Bring it to my place, it doesn't take long.

I'm feeling so hungry, where can it be?
I picture the food, they're bringing to me
Oh, there goes the phone
Who is it now?
Their car's broken down and I can't get my chow
I dream of a life without a car
But for now it's a dream
And it's tyres on tar!

Gillian Browning

YUPPIE LIVING

Internet, a way of life
The computer age
Chat room strife
The office a cage.

Mobile phones
Messages in text
People act like clones
Whatever will be next?

Films on disc DVD
Cameras digital
See what we see
We have our fill.

Shopping by computer
Micro Chips for tea
Inline silver scooter
Bar codes, nothing free.

Euro cash
Computer bin
E-mail trash
People commit computer sin.

Lap tops
Girls on tables
Using bar props
Showing navels.

Whizz kid yuppies
Too much money
Have mentality of puppies
Trying to be funny.

Football was working class game
A comment was made
Prawn sandwiches to blame
By the media brigade.

Commuters go by train
Pray for no crash
Often late, due to wrong kind of rain
Train buffet offers bangers and mash.

Smooth flow beer
What has happened to cask?
Makes people feel quite queer
Where have traditions gone?

It's called progress and overtaken
By *yuppie living!*

Chris Leggett

THE CHILD AND HER DOG

I have seen death on a bright sunny day,
A child and her grandmother passed my way
Walking along gently at their side
Was a little white dog, not likely to stray.

He was held by a lead
And as they passed by
The lead fell from the child's hand.
She gave a sharp cry.

The dog young and happy
Ran forward a pace
Found himself free
And started to race.

He dashed into the road
The grandmother turned round
What has happened here, oh dear?
She stood still.

The child in despair could not think what to do,
A moment before all happy and sweet
Now all was troublesome here in the street.

Alas for the two a lorry came into view
The little dog ran on trailing the lead
A dull thud and a quiver, and he lay still.
Dismay and shock as the two watched the deed
That would end their walk with the dog that day.

The lorry passed on and went on its way
The poor child ran to where the dog lay.
She picked him up and cradled him in her arms
And the two walkers I had seen on that brilliant day
Walked slowly and silently home and away.

Gladys Brunell

WHEN YOUNG AND HAPPY

'Charming and well mannered', read the advert
Just the man for me I said, but don't get hurt
Phone him right away, and make a date
Better hurry before it's too late
After meeting Charles we agreed to see a show
'You get the tickets,' he said to me, 'before we go.'
At the theatre we met at the door
He took me inside and said no more.
After the show I'd have liked to visit a cafe nearby
'Let's walk to your place,' he said as I gave a sigh
While he sat on the settee I made sandwiches and tea
'Leave the washing up,' he suggested, 'until tomorrow.'
Which only added to my sorrow.
After he left my heart did sink, but I began to think
What happened to my old friend Jack?
To pubs we would go, but going 'Dutch' to see a show.
No fuss we found, I knew when to buy a round
Except when Jack brought me chocolates in a box
And I replied, 'Bless his cotton socks.'
His flowers came with a kiss, I wouldn't miss
Meantime Charles phoned, 'Are we going out tonight?'
Sorry, a friend is in rather a plight
He just needs a pal to put him right.
He is taking me to see a show
No more walking, in a taxi we will go
There is no doubt, he will soon be about
Taking me here, there and everywhere
So now I'm full of fun at 25
And mean to stay happy and very much alive.

Eleanor Alderson

To A Fisherman's Love

As I gaze in at the coast through the morning haze
I wonder if you seawards gaze
How I wish you were here with me on this spring morn
To enjoy the beauty as the day is born
How lovely is the coast today with the mist rising from the bay
As the sun lifts the shroud from the ripening corn
It seems as if the land from the sea is drawn
The fields are bright, the houses with colour gay
Which cheers the heart after winter, long and grey
In the sun the white cliffs stand like castle walls, high and grand
My island home balanced on the green sea stands
Bedecked with ribbons of golden sand
My thoughts are of you this morning and I want to pass them on
So away I must scribble before they are gone
From my home shores I find it hard to stray
And from your side I hate to be away
Dear darling I say just once I love you, for if I said it a thousand times
It could not make my love deeper like snowflakes make the snow
I wish to see you happy with a smile upon your face,
But when we are not together
And I am out on the sea, I hope you are a little sadder
Because you are not with me.

Ronald Blay

I WISH

I wish the rain would go away
I wish the sun would stall all day
I wish the rain came overnight
And over its ownership one wouldn't fight.
I wish that peace will reign one day
And hope that some will come my way.
I wish for plenty of money to live
With lots left over with some to give.
I wish that people didn't have to judge
And wish that some wouldn't hold a grudge.
The world is large with room for all,
It's a shame that some feel the need to brawl.
I wish the world's food supply was plenty
And nobody had stomachs so empty.
If we could all get on in this human race,
The world would be a far better place.

Steve Elson

OUR NEW CAR

We've been saving now for quite a long time,
To buy a new car with a fresh new design.
It takes a long time to get all the money,
And really isn't all that sunny.

We've skimped and saved from dawn till dusk,
But it really, really is a must.
We think we'll have a sapphire blue,
As the colour's not common and that's true.

The day arrives that we've been hoping for,
To collect our new car and that's for sure.
Michael takes us for a ride to show,
The way she moves and takes it slow.

Bernard takes over the driving in a while,
And we go along in a lovely style.
The inside has air conditioning,
With the bodywork outside very glistening.

We drive back to the garage to settle the price,
To bring our car home will be very nice.
We say thank you very much and see you soon,
When the car needs a check-up we'll give you a phone.

Eileen Denham

My Wish...

A wish, a wish
Upon a star
A wish that
You are never far
Close to heart
Close to mind
The truest friend
I'll ever find.

Samantha Vaughan

REFLECTION!

It's nae aye gien
in the hindmaist end
ti cross yeir final 't'
nor e'en for some
o those faur ben,
tae eke thur braithe
for thur last 'Amen',
while neither an ane,
it seems tae me
is ready quite, for Eternity.
Were it gien tae Man
tae ken his time
tae sign himsel awaa -
was *noo*, nae hudden back,
nae time ataa for a last wee crack
nor dot the 'i's and cross the 't's
but get on his way nae mair ti say -
he'd still be hudden tichtly on
an sweir tae gang tae oblivion!
Sae God wha kens
His mak o Man
has gien him Life
wi a certain span.
He doesna staund
an wait for him
but caa's him in
as in days gaun by
when Man, himsel
ca'ed in the kye!

Andrew A Duncan

THE FOX

Fire light, fire bright,
Warming us on these cold nights,
The fox comes out of his warm lair
And sniffs the cold and frosty air,
Off he goes in jaunty mood
Foraging in bins for food.
Sniffing here, sniffing there,
Trying to sniff out some fine fare.
He looks up skyward to the moon
And hopes that he can go home soon
Then he spies my upturned bin
And I know that his luck's in.

Barbara Doel

TYRANNY

The king was a ruthless tyrant
Who sat upon his throne.
All manner of wrongful deeds
Were the ones he did condone.

His wicked ways were encouraged
By his equally wicked queen.
The schemes they planned together
Were the most dreadful ever seen.

Until one day a knight appeared,
So cheerful with all his songs,
With a quest bestowed in a far-off land
To rectify all the wrongs.

His clever plan was so superb
It made all the church bells ring.
By removing the queen with one deft move
He had checkmated the wretched king.

Laurence Idell

SMILE

Goodbye my friend
You come to me
Whenever the snow
Falls from the tree
When the sun is
In the sky
You peep through the clouds
And smile
When the flowers
Smile in the sun
Your eyes are warm
Like the sun.

Helen Owen

THE TRAUMA OF DEATH

As I wended my way home
At the end of my long day;
Just a para in my life, not a tome,
A colon in my colonic way.

Then my lazy dreams shattered as I saw
A police car, an ambulance, at my gate.
Then two men with bodied stretcher left my door:
And covered, it entered the ambulance in sorrow's state.

A policeman side-looked at me, and quoted duty.
'You must accompany me to our station,
And formally identify that is your wife's body.
I'm sorry, but that is the law of this nation.'

We arrived there and entered a room.
On a table the covered body in sorrow lay.
Around, stood officers in gloom,
Their faces portraying pity, all so grey.

Suddenly, my wife sat up alert.
Officers faces broke in mirth so gay.
'I'm sorry,' she said, 'I'm such a joking skirt:
But darling, have a happy, happy birthday!'

If you think this poem is just a trick,
Remember my wife's a helper in the nick.

J Collinson

CULTIVATORS IN JAMAICA

Scarf covering their heads
Shading from the fierce heat of the sun
Men and women working hard
Growing food crops for everyone.

Perspiration running down
Hard work is needed to grow food to nourish the body
Cultivators do not frown
Food required will need to be in plenty supply.

Maize, sweet potato, banana
Badoo, plantain, dashene, turnip
Ginger, peanut, cocoa, taya
Sugar cane, carrot, cassava and gynep.

Cashew and mango
Grapefruit
Yam and pimento
And more citrus fruits.

Science has been very useful
In the survival of mankind
To be healthy means to be careful;
Read published research on food
That is important for healthy body and mind.

In the search for progress in maintaining good health
Learning from our forefathers
Will not necessarily require wealth
But to practice good health matters.

Future generations learning about food cultivation
Will be pleased with our hand-me-down achievements
As they grow in admiration
We can appreciate their comments.

Olive May McIntosh-Stedman

LAKEHOUSE AND BEYOND

I needed the money, Val needed the help, we arranged to do a swop,
And so November '76, I went forth and used the mop.
The place was big, with many rooms, I hoped I'd cope quite well,
Val was nice and said to me, 'Don't worry, time will tell.'

With four big poodles at my feet and three hours ahead of me,
I started up the Hoover and was as busy as a bee.
The weeks sped by, our friendship grew and today it's hard to say,
Did I go three times a week, for friendship or for pay?

We shared the rough times and the smooth, we helped each other out.
A cup of tea, our little chats, I'll miss without a doubt.
Four years have passed, we've said goodbye, it's funny don't
                  you think?
I'll miss it all, the work as well, even wiping down the sink.

I left this work to marry Brian and work on the nursery with him.
Potting up bulbs, growing cut flowers and keeping the hedges trim.
Working the markets, out in all weathers, selling our home-grown
                  plants.
Struggling along to build up the business, admittedly with one or
                  two grants.

Sadly in 1989 I heard of the plight Val was in,
She'd had a big op, still in great pain and too weak to empty her bin.
So no more to do, off I flew and used all the elbow grease I could
                  muster.
I stayed this time six weeks until Val was well enough to use her duster.

We parted once more, got on with our lives, Val then moved 20
                  miles away.
Surprisingly through, 12 years later we met on that hot, June day.
Brian collapsed and died at the nursery, where together we'd worked
                  so hard,
And so now our friendship was reunited through a heartfelt sympathy
                  card.

I only go once a week now, but I've been back just over a year,
And yes, Val still has big poodles, but this time there's only a pair.
Familiar ornaments seem like old friends, bringing back such
                                                    happy times.
There's obviously new things as well as the old, in particular I like
                                                    the wind chimes.

Jennifer Hilling

LAMENT

'It's nearly the summer,' I thought.
'I can lay on that Lilo I bought.'
Then, I looked up and down
At myself, with a frown,
And wondered, 'Like this? Did I ought?'

My bikini will look very rum.
There's a great roll of fat round my tum!
Deary me! What's the use?
Though the top's gone all loose,
It's decidedly tight round my bum!

My skin looks all gooseflesh and wan
And my legs have all hair growing on.
I wish that I'd used
All the tips I perused
By the fire, when last summer'd gone!

If I'd rubbed some stuff into my skin
While the chance was there, I might have been
Such a sight to behold.
Smooth, slender and gold,
Instead of as ugly as sin!

I could lounge in the garden, I s'pose
And let the skin peel off my nose,
With my unsightly flesh
Hid from view by wire mesh
Which was put there for Bert's rambling rose.

Next year, I am going to try
To diet and jog and apply
All those advertised balms
That tone up your arms
And make all your cellulite die!

Anne Gardiner

COME THROUGH

Come through a hedge backwards
hair sticking up, like a hedgehog.

Sleeping a blustery blue winter
with gales whipping all around

the den where rest is sometimes
possible, though slow shaky it is,

glass rattling in its scruffy frame
setting the pointed teeth on edge.

Sometimes awake, in a grey fuzz
rubbing dry eyes, grip swallowing

razor-dry throat, heartbeats are
almost aching slow, living just, in

midst of a wild, sharp, dangerous
storm that has bomb-blown up all

safety, spreading lost leaves, stone,
trees all laying around, adrift on a

sea of amber, lifeless garden rubbish.
Then a wild, very weak watery sun

arises, struggling fiercely through the
soft grey clouds encircling in the sky,

to make its first bright, daring, dance
as spring's flighted, gold messenger.

Catherine Harris

THE CHOSEN ONE
(Mumtaz-i-Mahal)

It's dome the shape of a teardrop from a grieving eye
Soars white as a dove to the clear blue sky,
A rosy pink in the blush of dawn's early light
Like polar ice in the blue of velvet night.
Terraced gardens where fountains play
Cooling the air in the heat of the day,
The glistening waters reflect the shrine
Built to the memory of a love sublime.
The Taj Mahal is there for all to see,
Its story is part of India's history.

A million stars in the sky above
Shine down on this monument of an Emperor's love,
Twenty thousand toiled for more than twenty years,
And failed to ease his grief and tears,
Fourteen seeds of their love she bore,
Until her body could bear no more.
No opiate can ease the pain
Of the guilt that lurks within his brain,
With their last kiss he stole her dying breath
Then lay in his arms in the sleep of death.

His shoulders once so firm and straight
Now bowed by the worries and cares of state,
His cheeks are wet with bitter tears,
Her life cut short to so few years.
The Muezzin calls to prayer from the minaret,
But prayer cannot make heart and mind forget,
Her hair so soft and as dark as a raven's wings,
Her gentle voice in his ears still rings,
Is it her voice whispering, 'My love, my love!'
Or the distant sound of a cooing dove?

The prayer beads through his fingers slide,
His face betrays the grief inside,
Two of their sons by their brother slain,
The Mogul Empire's throne to gain.
With lines of grief etched on his face
He gazes at her resting place.
Deposed and broken he longs to die
Beside his beloved Arjumand then to lie,
Away from earthly grief and pain,
United with his beloved once again.

The Pure Of Heart Shall Enter The Garden Of God.
(Persian inscription carved over the entrance)

Thousands come to feast their eyes,
On this shrine an earthly paradise.
Very few men ever saw her face,
So how can we judge her beauty, her grace?
Only by gazing at this shrine an Emperor's dream,
Where lies his body and Arjumand his Queen.
This monument of a man and woman's love
Now united in a paradise above.

Roy Dickinson

FOOD HEAVEN

There's a special place for ladies
Where food never makes you fat
Calories have not been invented
As for cellulite - what's that?

Chocolate improves your complexion
A fry-up is good for your hair
Cream cakes are full of nutrition
Especially a chocolate eclair!

Chips are a daily essential
Puddings improve the mind
My favourite is jam roly-poly
The bigger the better, I find!

You must have plenty of custard
At least a litre or more
Followed by cheese and biscuits
A coffee and a petit four.

Whisky is good for your liver
Butter is good for your heart
Fried onions will aid your digestion
Followed by treacle tart!

That brings me back to custard
Made with sugar and cream
I know it's imagination
But surely a girl can dream!

Jackie Johnson

A FRIEND

Is friendship a hand upon a shoulder
Somewhere to hide for just a while?
A haven or shelter from life's rigors
Kind words and a comforting smile.

Or is friendship a time to be honest
To give and to take or to share?
Not just to mumble vague platitudes
But to be there and actually care.

Is friendship just merely acquaintance
Someone to drink with and lark?
Or is it the knowledge of true support
When times are so lonely and dark?

Is friendship a lifetime's performance
That must be re-enacted each day?
Or occasional times of great pleasure
A lone hand which helps you on your way?

A true friend's not a daily companion
Who will know all your problems and share
A real friend is one who despite miles and years
When you need them will always be there.

Though I may not see you each day now
You may slip from my thoughts for a while
If you call I'll be there to support you
Till on your own you can stand up and smile.

R Ansell

EARLY MORNING IN SIVOTA BAY

As I lie in my bunk I hear seconds tick by,
And I gaze through the hatch to a starry sky
That gazes back on the now silent sea,
On the bay, on the village, on the owls and on me.

Our now silent ship in the near silent bay
Will soon come alive with the noise of the day,
But the cocks that now to each other do crow
Will quieten themselves when the sun starts to grow.

The sun will soon raise each man and his wife
Who will work in the hills, as is their life,
And donkeys and goats and sheep I'll see
Climbing up through the hills away from the sea.

The raucous bray of the laden beast,
And the wind brought about by the fire in the east,
And the urgent noise of our children at play
Will change this still scene of our ship in the bay.

But now a few moments of silence I'll sip
With the owls and the stars and our little ship;
Before this dual scene is made one by the wind
I'll also reflect - both in sea and in mind.

Douglas Bryan Kennett

LEEDS

There was a young man from Leeds,
Who entered a race,
And couldn't keep up his speeds,
He lost his pace,
And had to admit his defeat,
When his shoes came off,
And had to run in his bare feet.

Hannah E Finnegan

SHREWSBURY

Wyle Cop, Dogpole, Mardol too,
All names of yesteryear,
Gives a stranger pleasant view
Of history, through ages here.

River Severn horseshoes all
With castle for the rest,
Church steeples show their tall,
Salopians truly blest.

Normans, Tudors, Cromwell's men,
All have left their mark,
For purposes right for when
Those days of yore were dark.

Darwin, Hill and Robert Clive
Are featured all in stone,
All have helped a nation strive,
Each one to his own.

Their statues look unseeingly
Across their part of town,
They gave their all unstintingly
Without so much a frown.

St Chads the church that fell apart,
Despite Telford's grim omen,
For now it was the time to start
And build again, as then.

Eddie Main

WHAT'S IN A NAME?

The name I was born with seems many years ago.
Has changed throughout the time span by the feelings people show.
Sometimes called by mother using ever letter true.
And sometimes in a shorter form, which I liked as it was new.
There have been many pet names quite a few I do recall.
And simple names when said by little children one and all.
By your children changed to Mother a very different form.
Meaning lovingness and guidance to keep them from all harm.
But now that nature brings the best, with a loving message sent.
For that is one I'll cling to - with which I am content.
To hold and value fondly for as long as e'er I can.
It's the name you utter to me when you call me Jackie Ann.

Dareni

THE HAPPY MAN

I saw the happy man today
Watching the children as they play
Smiling as they ran around
Listening to their every sound
He seemed to cherish every noise
Of all the laughing girls and boys

Why does he stand there every day
And watch them in this kind of way?
Does he remember distant times
Of children's games and playground rhymes?
Or is it thoughts of something more
That took him back to days of yore?

Maybe ghosts from out the past
Whose memory he knows will last
That he still sees within his mind
Or maybe age has just been kind
And gave him solace, peace and ease
And lovely childhood memories

I missed the happy man today
Someone said, 'He's gone away!'
I hope that where he is today
There's children laughing as they play
He can stand there with his smile
And watch the children for a while

Allan McFadyean

FRIENDSHIP

F riendships can begin in a casual way,
R abbiting over the garden fence,
I nteresting local gossip of the day,
E xpecting everything to make sense.
N ow a year later, firm friends we've become,
D eparture looms, for pastures new.
S ending letters and texts, but it won't be the same,
H opefully it's not long before I'm out of here too.
I care for and respect my neighbourhood mate,
P atient and kind, altogether - *just great!*

Elaine Carver